Piano • Vocal • Guitar

BEST OF Peter Tosh

Cover Photo: GAB Archive / Redferns / Getty Images

ISBN 978-1-4234-9220-7

HAL•LEONARD®
CORPORATION

7777 W. BLUEMOUND RD. P.O. BOX 13819 MILWAUKEE, WI 53213

Visit Hal Leonard Online at
www.halleonard.com

BRAND NEW SECOND HAND

Words and Music by
PETER TOSH

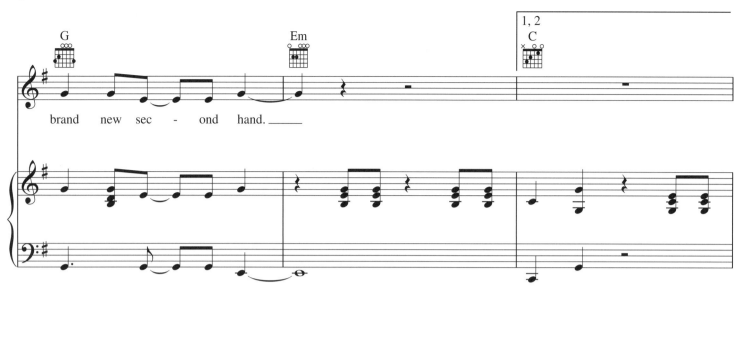

brand new sec - ond hand. _____

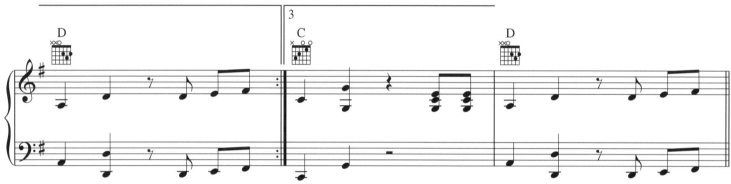

Repeat ad lib. and Fade

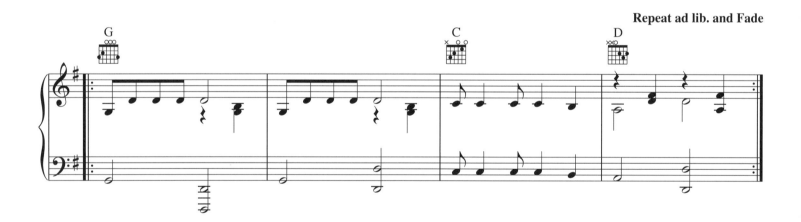

Additional Lyrics

2. You think it's the dress you wear that make you a lady,
   Get that out of your mind, girl, you must be crazy.
   Mama used to tell me, long time ago, girl,
   It's not everything you see glitter is gold.
   Chorus

3. See you watch them pass by, well, mighty tidy,
   But they don't know say it very nasty.
   Look Jaw your favours look how them tough,
   And Jaw-Bone favours banish down handcuff.
   Chorus

EQUAL RIGHTS

Words and Music by
PETER TOSH

Ev-'ry-one is cry-ing out __ for peace, yes. None is cry-ing out for

DOWNPRESSOR MAN

Words and Music by
PETER TOSH

Additional Lyrics

4. I wouldn't like to be a flea
   Under your collar man
   I wouldn't like to be a flea
   Under your collar man
   I wouldn't like to be a flea
   Under your collar man
   All along that day

5. You can run but you can't hide
   You can run but you can't hide
   You can run but you can't hide
   Telling you all along that day

6. You gonna run to the Lord
   Beggin' to hide you
   You gonna run to the Lord
   Beggin' to hide you
   You gonna run to the Lord
   Beggin' to hide you
   You gonna run to Jah
   Beggin' to hide you
   All, all along that day

GET UP STAND UP

Words and Music by BOB MARLEY
and PETER TOSH

Get up, stand up, don't give up __ the fight.
Get up, stand up, don't give up __ the fight.
Get up, stand up, don't give up __ the fight. We're

Preach - er man, don't tell __ me __ heav - en is un - der the earth. __
Most peo - ple think __ great God will come __ from the sky, __
sick and tired of your is - m and skism game. Die and go to heav - en in Je - sus' name, Lord.

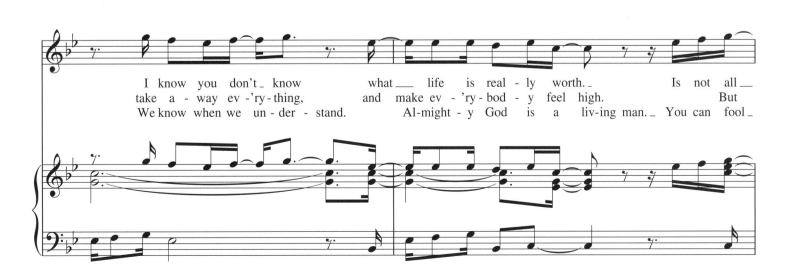

I know you don't __ know what __ life is real - ly worth. __ Is not all __
take a - way ev -'ry-thing, and make ev -'ry-bod - y feel high. But
We know when we un - der - stand. Al-might - y God is a liv-ing man. __ You can fool __

STEPPIN' RAZOR

Words and Music by
JOE HIGGS

Half-time Reggae feel

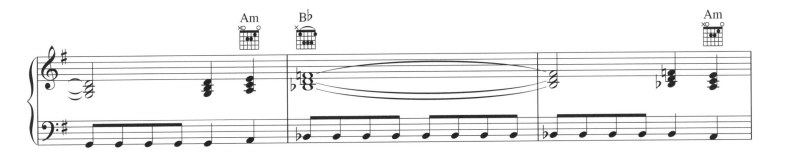

1. If you want to live,
2.-7. (See additional lyrics)

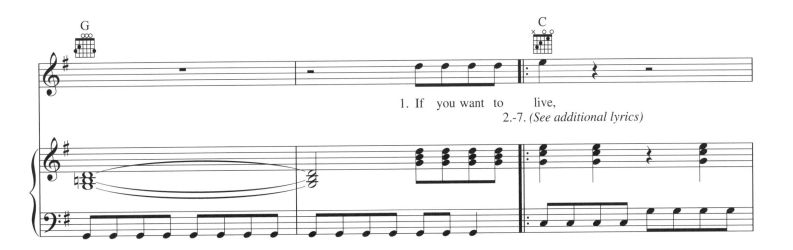

treat ___ me ___ good.   If you want to

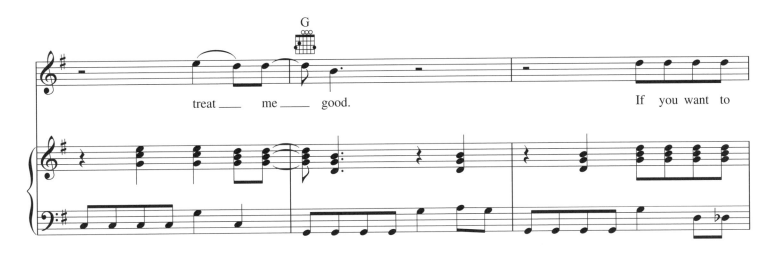

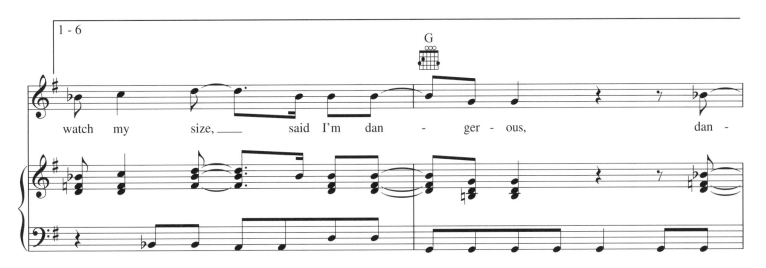

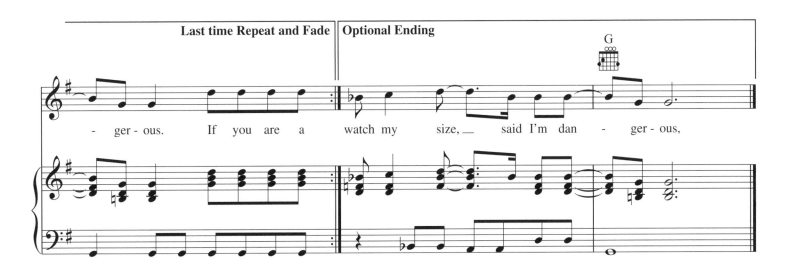

Additional Lyrics

2. If you are a bully
   Treat me good
   If you are a bully, a bully
   I beg you treat me good
   I'm like a steppin' razor,
   Chorus

3. If you are a chucky
   Nobody chucky from me
   If you are a chucky, a chucky
   Nobody chuck from me, yeah
   I'm like a steppin' razor,
   Chorus

4. If you eat asphalt
   I beg you treat me good
   If you drink lead soup
   You better treat me good
   I'm like a steppin' razor,
   Chorus

5. If you are bull bukka
   Nobody buk from me
   If you are duppy
   You move away from me
   I'm like a steppin' razor,
   Chorus

6. If you want to live
   Treat me good
   Warning you, if you want to live
   You better treat me good
   I'm like a steppin' razor,
   Chorus

7. If you drink mortar
   Treat me good
   And if you eat brick
   Treat me good
   I'm like a steppin' razor,
   Chorus

KETCHY SHUBY

Words and Music by
PETER TOSH

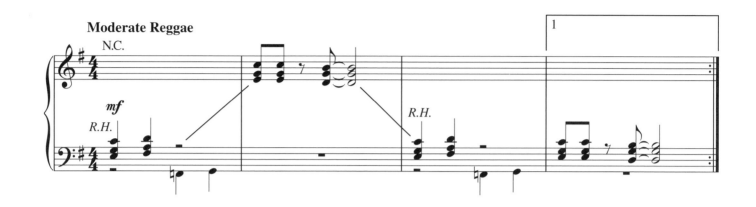

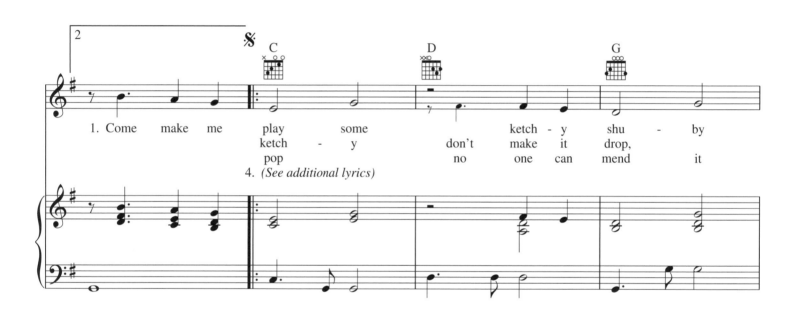

1. Come make me play some ketch-y shu-by
   ketch-y don't make it drop,
   pop no one can mend it
   4. *(See additional lyrics)*

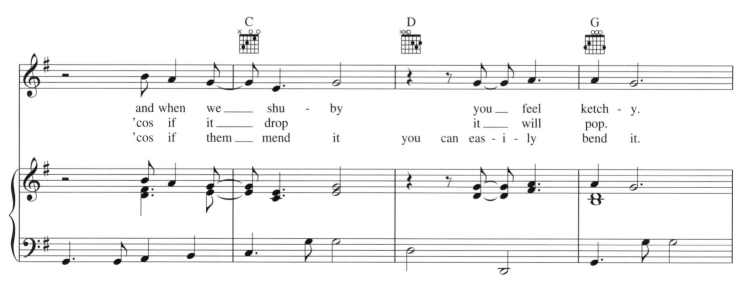

and when we ___ shu-by you ___ feel ketch-y.
'cos if it ___ drop it ___ will pop.
'cos if them ___ mend it you can eas-i-ly bend it.

Additional Lyrics

4. It don't take too long to learn,
   Just do as I say.
   It may take one hour or two,
   But the next time you will know.

LEGALIZE IT

Words and Music by
PETER TOSH

Moderate Reggae

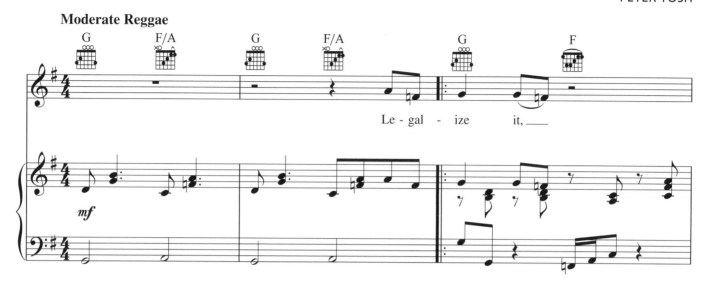

Le - gal - ize it, ___

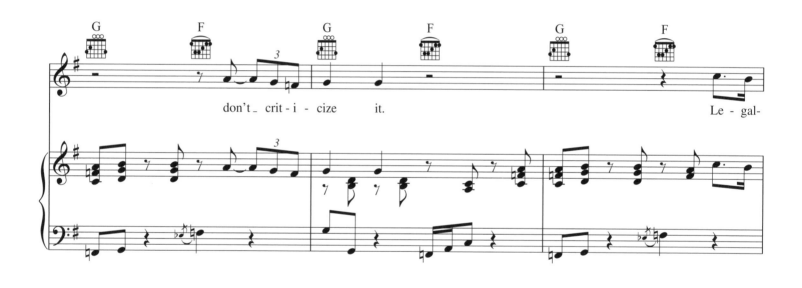

don't _ crit - i - cize it. Le - gal-

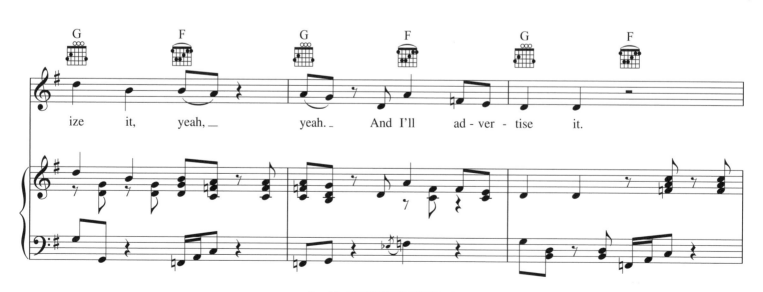

ize it, yeah, ___ yeah. _ And I'll ad - ver - tise it.

33

NO SYMPATHY

Words and Music by
PETER TOSH

Additional Lyrics

2. Might as well, might as well, yeah,
I get out, I get out of here.
Hell could never be made for me,
So I'm gonna search, search till I no feel.

TILL YOUR WELL RUNS DRY

Words and Music by
PETER TOSH

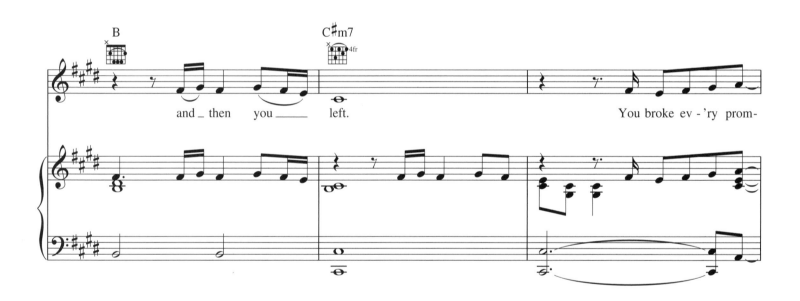

Additional Lyrics

Verse 2: Listen to me, darling, you're cheating me lie.
Now you came a running, wanting a second try.
You never miss your water till your well runs dry.

Chorus 2: Tell me, tell me, what you gonna do when you're feeling blue?
What you gonna do (oh my my) when you're feeling blue?
What you gonna do when you're feeling so blue?

Verse 3: Sat down inside and I heard you're racking.
I watched you pass by me, but you said nothing, not one single word.
But I know you're gonna miss me and you're gonna be blue.

WHY MUST I CRY

Words and Music by PETER TOSH
and BOB MARLEY

WHATCHA GONNA DO

Words and Music by
PETER TOSH

Additional Lyrics

2. Next week, next week is the case.
   I'm 'ave a draped judge to face.
   I'm 'ave the island sea in space,
   Or make the doctor man work on his face.
   Chorus

3. Next-door neighbor, them 'old your son.
   They say they find him with one gun.
   And there's no need to mention,
   I'm going to get an indefinite detention.
   Chorus

4. I'm no nobody,
   So 'im mus' here remain in custody.
   I'm see Babylon and stand up and screw,
   Say, 'im never knew was a curfew.
   Chorus